FROM CHAOS TO CLARITY

THE SIMPLEST STORY EVER TOLD

Wayne C. Kellis

WESTBOW
PRESS®
A DIVISION OF THOMAS NELSON
& ZONDERVAN

All Scriptures quoted were taken from THE HOLY BIBLE, NEW INTERNATIONAL VERSION®, NIV® Copyright © 1973, 1978, 1984, 2011 by Biblica, Inc.® Used by permission. All rights reserved worldwide.

WestBow Press books may be ordered through booksellers or by contacting:

WestBow Press
A Division of Thomas Nelson & Zondervan
1663 Liberty Drive
Bloomington, IN 47403
www.westbowpress.com
1 (866) 928-1240

Because of the dynamic nature of the Internet, any web addresses or links contained in this book may have changed since publication and may no longer be valid. The views expressed in this work are solely those of the author and do not necessarily reflect the views of the publisher, and the publisher hereby disclaims any responsibility for them.

Any people depicted in stock imagery provided by Thinkstock are models, and such images are being used for illustrative purposes only.

Certain stock imagery © Thinkstock.

ISBN: 978-1-4497-3405-3 (sc)
ISBN: 978-1-4497-3404-6 (e)

Library of Congress Control Number: 2011962535

Print information available on the last page.

WestBow Press rev. date: 11/22/2017

Dedicated to

Zack, Kristy, Lynden & Kylie

Teach your children
to love Jesus

TABLE OF CONTENTS

FOREWORD

Despite having grown up in a church that highly values God's word, attending Bible camps, a Christian college, Bible studies, and having personal study time, I have always struggled with having a clear understanding of the Bible. Given the difference in cultures, time periods, and multiple story lines, it is not hard to understand my dilemma. Having talked to many other people, I believe this is not uncommon.

For my 25th birthday I asked my Dad to write a simple summary of the Bible. It is not intended to replace or be a substitute for God's word but it is meant to be used as a tool to help me (and others) grasp the context of the Bible. By far, this is the best birthday present ever.

I am so thankful for this book as it has already helped me to learn more about our amazing God. I hope you find it as beneficial as I do.

Love In Christ,
Kylie Kellis Myers

INTRODUCTION

The purpose of this account of the main storyline of the Bible is to help the reader to know and to understand the story. Many people are unnecessarily intimidated by the Bible. Even though they may have heard or read stories from the Bible, they have never really understood how it all fits together. They may be confused about which Biblical characters come first chronologically, how they are related, or the order of events. The fact that the Bible has been shrouded in mystery only adds to this confusion. God's message to mankind was never meant to be hidden or difficult to understand. As a nation, we have gotten so far from serious study of the scriptures that it seems we are now overwhelmed by the idea of actually understanding them. This writing will not replace careful, prayerful study of God's word to mankind, but it is my hope and prayer that this account will remove some of the confusion that surrounds this greatest of all books.

It is true that the Bible is so rich and so deep that a lifetime of serious study would not be adequate to mine its riches. No one will ever fully comprehend all that is taught in this book. The amazing thing is that a book so rich and so deep can, on another level, really be quite simple. The person of average abilities can grasp the story in sufficient measure, but the highest intellect will never fully grasp it all. So, you should not be discouraged if you do not understand it all immediately. It is truly an amazing book. The Bible is God's love revealed and truly is the simplest story ever told.

As we begin, it is important to point out that the Bible is not written as a rule book. The majority of it is narrative. It tells a story of love, violence, wrath, mercy, separation and redemption. Our task is to understand the story and make application as we are able.

The Old Testament

THE CREATION STORY
(Genesis Chapters 1-2)

There is a great deal of debate over the first few chapters of Genesis. The book opens with the statement that *"In the beginning God created the heavens and the earth."* This statement alone was revolutionary for its time. The significance of this statement is that there is one God. Most cultures were polytheistic and worshiped many gods.

The creation story is told in the first two chapters. Many questions have been raised about this section of scripture. Is the creation story allegory? Were the six days of creation really only six twenty-four hour days? There are many unanswerable questions, but we should not get bogged down in issues of this sort. What we need to take away from the creation accounts is that one God created the world, and that He created man, as His crowning achievement, in His own image.

Unlike the creation stories found in mythology, the biblical story of creation makes no attempt to explain where God comes from. It is assumed that the Creator was always there. Likewise there is no attempt to explain where the matter used in creation came from. God created *ex nihilo* (Latin for "out of nothing") as he simply spoke the universe—time, matter, energy, laws of physics and chemistry—into existence. All other creation stories try to explain where the creating deity originated or what he (or she) used in creating. The point we should not overlook is that the Bible stands alone in maintaining that God has always been and that there was nothing in existence until He created it.

It is interesting to note that God says *"Let us make man in our image."* It is clear that there is only one God. Yet somehow God the Father, Jesus the Son, and God's Spirit are all God. One more note before we move on: God is not known as "our Father" until Jesus refers to Him in this way.

THE FALL
(Genesis Chapter 3)

After creation, Adam and Eve enjoyed fellowship with God for an unspecified period of time. They were free to eat from any tree in the Garden of Eden except from the tree of the knowledge of good and evil. In the course of time, Satan, appearing as a serpent, appealed to Eve's pride and convinced her to eat the forbidden fruit. Eve gave some to Adam, who was with her, and he ate. Sin has entered the world and things will never be the same. Adam and Eve become conscious of their nakedness, hide from God, and suffer many hardships as a result of their sin.

We were created to live in a relationship with God. Yet sin (disobedience to God) separates mankind from the Creator. The problem is that man has broken the relationship and is unable to repair it. God cannot have fellowship with man in his sinful state. So, God takes it upon Himself to repair the relationship by paying the price Himself. God worked this out in a way that did not interfere with mankind's free will or His (God's) holy and just nature. Sin seems inevitable in that God only gives one command to be obeyed, but Adam and Eve could not keep even the one. Yet the story of the Garden makes it clear that it was a free choice to disobey God that led to separation and expulsion. In some way that is difficult to understand, all Creation, not just mankind, is affected, left in this fallen state as a result of Adam and Eve's disobedience until God redeems everything at His chosen time.

It is impossible to know just how fallen we really are. Paul states in Romans 8:22, *"We know that the whole creation has been groaning as in the pains of childbirth right up to the present time."* Very early in scripture, God hints at His love for us that will be manifested in our redemption. In Genesis 3:15 God says to Satan, *"And I will put enmity between you and the woman, and between your offspring and hers; he will crush your head, and you will strike his heel."* This is a reference to the work of Jesus on the cross. Satan will strike at Him, but He will crush Satan.

Already, the story of the gospel is in view.

CAIN AND ABEL
(Genesis Chapter 4)

Adam and Eve's first two sons were Cain and Abel. Out of jealousy, Cain killed Abel. This is the first murder in the Bible. So that no one would harm him, God put a mark on Cain and sent him away. Even in the case of murder, God showed his merciful desire to redeem man.

THE FLOOD
(Genesis Chapters 6-9)

A sad statement is made in Genesis 6:5: *"The LORD saw how great the wickedness of the human race had become on the earth, and that every inclination of the thoughts of the human heart was only evil all the time."* Mankind had reached the depths of depravity and verse 6 says, *"The LORD regretted that he had made human beings on the earth, and his heart was deeply troubled."*

God found one righteous man by whom He would deliver mankind. I hope that you can see a glimmer of Jesus in this story. Noah and his family built an Ark and floated on the waters for about a year. When he got off the Ark, he built an altar and sacrificed to the Lord. God made a covenant with Noah that He would not destroy mankind by water again. As a sign of the covenant, He put the rainbow in the sky. A covenant is just a two-party agreement, similar to a contract, which contains certain promises and establishes a relationship. The idea behind covenants is an important Biblical principle. In fact the word "testament" (as in Old Testament and New Testament) is just another word for "covenant."

THE TOWER OF BABEL
(Genesis Chapter 11)

Noah's descendants survived to repopulate the world, and everyone spoke the same language. They began to build a tower to the heavens. God saw what they were doing and concluded that if they continued to speak the same language and work together, then nothing they attempted would be impossible for them. God scattered them all over the earth and they stopped building. I am sure there is a great deal to learn about what can be accomplished when everyone "speaks the same language and works together."

THE PATRIARCHS
(Genesis Chapters 12-50)

ABRAHAM
(Genesis Chapters 12-25)

The rest of the Bible follows the life of the family of one man. Through this man's family, God will bring about the redemption of humanity. God calls Abram (later changed to Abraham) out of Ur. He was told to *"go to a land that I will show you."* God made Abraham a series of promises:

1. I will make of you a great nation.
2. I will make your name great and you will be a blessing.
3. All the people of the earth will be blessed through you.

Later on, it will become clear that the last of these promises is another reference to God's plan to redeem all of mankind through Jesus, who according to his human family was a direct descendant of Abraham.

Abram's response in obeying God's command to leave his home and just "go" is the first of many demonstrations of his faithfulness. The decision could not have been an easy one. He was a rich man with no real reason to go anywhere. It is also possible that he was completely unfamiliar with this God who was suddenly calling him. The area where he was from was known for idol worship, and there is no indication in the text that Abram and God had any prior relationship before this call to "go." One thing is certain, Abram's faithful response to God stands in contrast to Adam and Eve's disobedience and sets the stage for the remainder of the Bible story. God could have worked out His will without Abraham's participation, but the story would have been completely different without him and his family in it.

Abraham's nephew Lot went with him. Lot's family and possessions grew to the point that he had to separate from Abraham. He moved to Sodom. When the wickedness in Sodom grew so bad that God decided to destroy it, He revealed His plan to Abraham. Abraham pleaded with God not to destroy the righteous with the wicked, and Lot and his two daughters were rescued.

When God destroyed the cities of Sodom and Gomorrah, Lot's wife was turned into a pillar of salt. The Bible says that she *"looked back."* We are forced to wonder why such a penalty was attached to simply looking back. The word used for "looked back" in Hebrew carries with it the idea of looking back longingly. It seems that Lot's wife loved the city and the life she had experienced there.

Lot's daughters successfully plotted to get him drunk and have sex with him in order to preserve their family line. The depravity inherent in the idea is troubling, but we must remember that these women grew up in Sodom. We should learn that exposing ourselves to what the wicked consider normal can have lasting, damaging influence.

The children born of these unions were Moab and Ammon. These became the Moabites and Ammonites that later caused trouble for the nation of Israel.

Because Abraham and Sarah were childless, their belief in God's promise to make Abraham into a great nation required faith indeed. Abraham is known for his great faith; still, there are a few instances when even he suffered from doubt and a lack of faith. Twice Abraham told people that Sarah was his sister because he was afraid they would kill him in order to have Sarah. In one case, God appeared to the king that Abraham had lied to. God told him, *"You are as good as dead because of the woman you have taken."* As it turned out, he had not come near Sarah and defended himself saying that Abraham had told him that Sarah was his sister. God responded that He knew this, and the reason He had appeared in a dream was to keep the king from sinning.

There are a couple of ideas that should be taken from this story:
1. We should be slow to assume the character of others will be lower than our own.
2. We should not forget that God is not only concerned with us but cares about others as well.

Nevertheless, God took Abraham on a faith building journey throughout his life. God later repeated His promise to Abraham, and Abraham reminded God that he had no son. When God said that He would indeed give him a son, Abraham believed God, and his faith was *"credited to him as righteousness."* (Genesis 15:6) This statement will become an essential key to the Christian understanding of righteousness. The Bible says that Abraham was made righteous when God credited righteousness to him based on faith. Abraham was not yet circumcised, did not have the law, and did not achieve righteousness by works. Roughly 2,000 years later, Paul will make much of these facts in his letter to the Romans. (See Romans 4:1-24 and Galatians 3:6-9) Paul makes the argument that God will credit us with righteousness, based on faith in Jesus Christ, just as He credited righteousness to Abraham.

Abraham and Sarah still have no children. At one point, when they were approaching the end of any possible childbearing age, Sarah suggested that Abraham have a son with Hagar, Sarah's servant. Ishmael was the son of this union. When Ishmael was a young boy, God commanded that Abraham and his household be circumcised as a sign of the covenant He had made with Abraham.

God waited until Sarah was well past the age of child bearing. He then appeared to Abraham and told him that Sarah would have a son at the same time next year. Sarah laughed. Isaac (his name means laughter) was born according to the promise. In Galatians, Paul will make the connection that Christians are like Isaac, the child of the promise, and that the Jews are like Ishmael, the child of the slave woman.

When Isaac was a young man, God told Abraham to sacrifice his son on a mountain in Moriah. Abraham did not hesitate to obey. He reasoned that God could bring Isaac back to life. When they arrived at the base of the mountain, Abraham told his servants, *"Wait here, the boy and I will go to the mountain to worship and we will return."* We should note that even though Abraham was prepared to sacrifice Isaac, he had faith that somehow both he and Isaac would return. Abraham bound Isaac and was about to kill him when an angel stopped him. God stopped Abraham from sacrificing his son, but God actually sacrificed His only son Jesus for us.

ISAAC

After the death of Sarah, Abraham sent his servant back to their homeland to secure a wife for Isaac. God made the journey successful, and the servant returned with Rebecca who became Isaac's wife. We do not read as much about Isaac as we do Abraham and Joseph. He did at times suffer from a lack of courage or faith just like his father Abraham. Isaac also told Abimelech that Rebecca was his sister. He did this out of fear that someone would kill him because his wife was beautiful. Abimelech saw Isaac caressing Rebecca and realized that she was his wife. In the end Abimelech proved to be a man of integrity, giving protection to Isaac and Rebecca.

JACOB AND ESAU

In time, Isaac and Rebecca had twin boys whom they named Jacob and Esau. Jacob was born second, and he came out holding to the heel of Esau. Jacob's name means "supplanter." As it will turn out, this is exactly his character. Esau grew up and became a skilled hunter. He was a rough, outdoors, manly man. Jacob was the type of guy who hung around the house and enjoyed cooking. Their parents chose favorites. Not surprisingly, Isaac loved Esau, and Rebecca loved Jacob.

Since Esau was born first, he was entitled to the birthright. The birthright was a custom that provided a double share of the inheritance to the firstborn. In this case, it meant that Esau would receive two thirds and Jacob would receive one third. Isaac was a wealthy man, so the birthright was an important thing. One day after Esau had been out hunting, he came home hungry. Jacob had prepared some food and offered to give some to Esau in exchange for his birthright. Esau took the deal and traded his birthright for what was, essentially, a bowl of soup. This incident sheds light on the character of both men at this time in their lives.

Later, Rebecca also devised a plan with Jacob to steal Isaac's blessing that was intended for Esau. The plan worked. Jacob and Rebecca deceived the now blind Isaac into blessing Jacob instead of Esau. Feel the poignancy of Isaac's blessing from Genesis 27:

"May God give you of heaven's dew and of earth's richness—an abundance of grain and new wine. [29]

*May nations serve you and peoples bow down to you.
Be lord over your brothers, and may the sons of your
mother bow down to you. May those who curse you be
cursed and those who bless you be blessed."*

Did you notice the piercing references to being
"lord over his brothers" and his *"mother's sons?"* No
wonder Esau vowed to kill Jacob! Jacob fled to his
mother's family. Here he went to work for his uncle
Laban. He fell in love with his cousin Rachael and
worked seven years in exchange for the right to take
her for a wife. On his wedding night, he discovered
he had actually married Rachael's older sister Leah.
He worked another seven years for Rachael and
ended up with two wives.

Leah began to give birth to children, but Rachel
did not. Jealousy caused Rachael to give her hand
maiden to Jacob to provide children. This caused
Leah to also give her hand maiden to Jacob to
provide more children. Finally, Rachael gave birth
to two children of her own. They were Joseph and
Benjamin. Naturally, these two were Jacob's favorites
because their mother was his favorite wife. In total,
Jacob had twelve sons from whom the twelve tribes
of Israel eventually would come. These tribes were
simply extended families. The twelve brothers are
commonly referred to as the "Patriarchs," a word that
simply means "Fathers."

God caused Jacob to prosper, and over time he became wealthy. When he realized that Laban was continuing to deal dishonestly with him, he took his family and possessions and went back to his home. He was afraid of how Esau might receive him, but Esau welcomed him back. One night on his trip back home, Jacob wrestled with "a man" all night long. Jacob would not let the "man" go until He blessed him. The "man" (Angel of the Lord?) touched Jacob in the hip, giving him a permanent limp. Jacob's name was changed to Israel because he had wrestled with God and overcome. This incident is symbolic of Israel's life. He started out as a dishonest, deceiving man but became an upright, God fearing man.

JOSEPH AND HIS BROTHERS

There are many references to the tribes of Israel in the Bible. As noted above, the twelve tribes are the families of the twelve sons of Israel. If you pay close attention, you will notice that the names of the tribes vary a little from one list to another. Most of the confusion is caused by the fact that near the end of his life, Israel essentially adopts Joseph's two sons, Ephraim and Manasseh. When the nation finally takes the land of Canaan, the land is divided into twelve portions. Ephraim and Manasseh each inherit portions. In essence, the family of Joseph receives the double portion.

The tribe of Levi does not receive land. They were designated as the priestly tribe, lived among all of the people and were to be supported by the offerings made to God.

Joseph was the oldest son of his father's favorite wife. He was clearly his father's favorite son and his ten older brothers were jealous of him. They sold him to some traveling traders who took Joseph and sold him into slavery in Egypt. The brothers killed an animal and put its blood on Joseph's coat. When they got back home, they all deceived their father by telling him that the blood stained coat was all they had found of Joseph.

If we pay attention, it is hard to miss the favoritism and deceit that runs in this family. It carries from one generation to the next and seems to grow in severity. A more modern and frequently used term is "dysfunctional."

Joseph was sold to a prominent Egyptian named Potiphar. He quickly became trusted and rose to prominence in Potiphar's house. One day, Potiphar's wife came in and tried to force Joseph to go to bed with her. She held onto his robe when he ran from the house. Out of revenge Potiphar's wife accused Joseph of attempting to rape her, and he was thrown into prison.

Joseph was in prison with the Pharaoh's cupbearer and baker. They each had dreams that Joseph interpreted for them. The interpretations revealed that the cupbearer was to be restored to his position, but the baker was to be beheaded. Both interpretations proved to be true.

Two years later, Pharaoh had a dream that no one could interpret. The cupbearer remembered Joseph and told the king that he could interpret the dream. Joseph was brought from prison and interpreted the dream to mean that there would be seven years of plenty followed by seven years of famine in Egypt. Joseph advised the Pharaoh of some ways of dealing with the coming famine, and Pharaoh was so impressed he promoted Joseph to second in command in all of Egypt.

To prepare for the famine, Joseph had the nation store up grain during the seven years of plenty. When the famine came, there was plenty of food in Egypt. However, in Canaan, where Joseph's family lived, the famine was severe. When the family ran out of food, Israel (formerly Jacob) sent ten of his sons (not including Benjamin) to buy food in Egypt. When they arrived, Joseph recognized his brothers, but they did not recognize him. When they left, Joseph demanded that they bring their youngest brother Benjamin back with them to prove they were not spies. He had Simeon bound and kept until they could bring Benjamin. Joseph also had the money for the food put back into their sacks. When they ran out of food again, Benjamin had to go with his brothers back to Egypt. This time, Joseph had his silver cup put in Benjamin's sack. Once the brothers had headed back home, Joseph sent men after them who found the cup in Benjamin's sack. (Remember, Benjamin is the new favorite of their father.)

Joseph said that all of the brothers were free to go, but Benjamin would stay and become his slave. At this, Judah begged Joseph to take him as a slave and let Benjamin go back to his father because his father had already lost one son and his life is closely bound to Benjamin. Judah (and we have to suppose all of the brothers) was now more concerned about his brother and his father than he was about his own life. It is clear that this episode is recorded in such detail to point out the astonishing change in these men. The situation was the same. Ten brothers had a younger brother whom their father preferred. Now they had an opportunity to get rid of this one too. This time, however, they chose the better course of action and placed the interests of their younger brother Benjamin ahead of their own.

Joseph revealed himself to his brothers and told them not to be concerned. He had the wisdom to see that even though his brothers had intended him harm, it was God who was using it all to work out the salvation of His chosen family during this time of famine. Once again, we see God providing for the redemption of His people.

Joseph sent carts back with his brothers to bring Israel and all of his possessions to Egypt. The idea seemed to be that they were only going to stay until the famine ended. Israel and his entire family continued to live in Egypt even after the famine was over. The book of Genesis ends with the death of Israel. It would be around 400 years before God would bring the Israelites out of Egypt.

JOB

Job is a book that I do not believe can be dated. Job is a deeply theological book about suffering that is difficult to understand but well worth reading and thinking about. I comment on it here because the events of this book could have occurred before the time of Abraham. This book tells the story of a faithful, wealthy man of God who suffers great loss at the hands of Satan, endures the judgment of his friends, eventually questions God, is questioned by God, yet remains faithful. In the end, God causes him to prosper even more than before.

EXODUS, LEVITICUS, NUMBERS AND DEUTERONOMY

These books record the period of time in which Moses lived. There is some duplication of events in these accounts but generally speaking, Exodus tells the story of Moses' life, the exodus of the Israelites from Egypt, the giving of the law and the forty years spent wandering in the desert. Leviticus primarily focuses on the law. The book of Numbers deals with numbering the families of Israel and Deuteronomy is a retelling of the law and some of the events that occurred during the life of Moses.

MOSES, THE EXODUS AND THE GIVING OF THE LAW

The Israelites, as the descendants of Israel came to be known, prospered in Egypt for around 400 years. Eventually, they became so numerous that some of the Egyptians began to fear them. This led to the enslavement of all of the Israelites. When the conditions became unbearable, they called out to the God of their Fathers for deliverance.

The book of Exodus, as its title suggests, tells the story of the Israelites' exodus from Egypt. It opens with the story of Moses' birth.

Moses was born at a time when the Egyptians lived in fear of the fact that the Israelites were becoming too numerous. Pharaoh ordered that all newborn male children be destroyed. When Moses was born, his parents placed him in a basket in the river in hopes of saving his life. Moses' sister was watching to see what would become of him and saw the Pharaoh's daughter rescue Moses. Moses' sister suggested to Pharaoh's daughter that she should find one of the Hebrew women to care for the child. Pharaoh's daughter agreed. With permission, she got Moses' own mother to come to the home of Pharaoh's daughter and care for him. Moses ended up being raised as royalty but cared for by his own mother.

When Moses was 40 years old, he thought the Israelites could see that God would use him to deliver the nation from bondage. One day he witnessed an Egyptian beating an Israelite. Moses killed the Egyptian and hid his body. The next day, he came across two Israelites fighting each other. When he intervened, one of the men asked him if he was going to kill them like he did the Egyptian. When Moses realized the murder was known, he fled to Midian.

In Midian, he met and married the daughter of Jethro. Moses spent the next 40 years tending sheep in Midian. One day he noticed a bush that was on fire but was not being consumed. God spoke to

Moses from the burning bush and instructed him to go to Pharaoh and demand that he let God's people go. Moses was reluctant and offered several reasons why he was not the man for the job. Moses' lack of faith angered God, but in the end God told Moses to take his brother Aaron along to do the speaking for him.

It is interesting to note that when the younger Moses assumed he was ready and that God would clearly use him, God was not ready to do so. Perhaps Moses was just not ready or perhaps God uses those who do not think quite so highly of themselves. God used the 40 years of tending sheep in Midian to develop the qualities of a shepherd in Moses. This prepared him to lead the people out of Egypt.

When Moses demanded that Pharaoh let the Israelites go, the Bible tells us, Pharaoh's heart was hardened. God brought a series of ten plagues on Egypt in an attempt to convince Pharaoh to let the people go.

The final plague was the death of the firstborn in all the land. The Israelites were able to escape this plague by killing lambs and applying the lambs' blood to the sides and tops of the door frames of their houses. The Lord said He would *"pass over"* the houses that had the blood applied to them.

This event is the historical basis for the Jewish feast known as Pesach, or Passover. It was this feast that Jesus would later partake of when He declared the bread represented His body and the wine represented His blood. During this meal, He instructed His disciples to *"do this in remembrance of Me."* We memorialize this event today when we partake of the Lord's Supper and recall the life, death, burial and resurrection of our Lord Jesus Christ.

The point that we should not miss is that the deliverance from death in Egypt was brought about by the blood of an innocent sacrifice for those who had applied it. This event, celebrated by the Israelites and their descendants as the feast of Passover, was always meant to be a picture of the deliverance of Christians who escape spiritual death by the blood of another innocent sacrifice, Jesus Christ.

When all of the firstborn in Egypt died, Pharaoh at first let the Israelites go. However he quickly changed his mind and sent his army after them. Moses and the nation came to a halt at the Red Sea while Pharaoh's army was coming up behind them. The Israelites were trapped. Moses stretched his rod out over the sea and it separated. The Israelites walked across on dry land. When the army followed, the waters swallowed them, and they all drowned.

Moses led the nation to Mount Sinai where God called him up on the mountain. While Moses was on the mountain, God wrote the Ten Commandments on two tablets of stone. Moses was gone for a long time and the people thought he might not come back. To pacify the people, Aaron had them make a golden calf to worship.

When Moses came back down from the mountain and saw that the people were worshiping the calf, he broke the tablets, ground the calf to dust, and made the people drink it in their water.

Moses went back onto the mountain, and God wrote the commandments on two more stone tablets. While he was on the mountain, Moses was instructed in all of the law. Once he came down, he delivered the Law (Torah in Hebrew) to the nation. All of the people agreed to it. Israel was intended to be a Theocracy (God would also be their King).

The Law governed the religious and social lives of the people. It is this Law that Jesus obeyed perfectly. Because He did this, He was without sin and innocent, a perfect sacrifice who could give His life for ours. He did not deserve to die but chose to die in order that we might live.

God had long ago promised the Land of Canaan to Abraham's descendants. They had lived there from the time of Abraham until Israel and his family moved to Egypt to escape the famine. It had been 400 years since this family had lived in Canaan. Now it was time to take the land back.

Moses sent twelve men to Canaan to spy out the land. Ten of the spies returned with a very disheartening report. They said it was a very good land but the people there were like giants and could not be defeated. Two of the spies, Joshua and Caleb, disagreed and said they could take the land, but the Israelites would not be convinced.

Because of their lack of faith, God made the nation wander in the desert for 40 years until the faithless generation died. The only people over 20 years old that came out of Egypt and went into the land of Canaan (the Promised Land) were Joshua and Caleb, the two spies who had wanted to take the land 40 years earlier. During these years of wandering, the people continually grumbled and complained. God provided for them by sending manna and quail to eat, but still they complained.

Joshua and the Conquest of Canaan

When God was ready for them to take the land, He did not allow Moses to enter. When God had told Moses to speak to a rock to get water to flow from it, he instead struck the rock. The punishment was that he would not enter the Promised Land. Moses went up on a mountain that overlooked Canaan and there he died.

Joshua became the new leader of the people. He led the people during the conquest of Canaan which lasted for a few years. This story is recorded in the book of **Joshua**.

One of the most famous events of this period was the battle of Jericho. Joshua had sent some spies into Jericho. They went to the house of Rahab, a prostitute. She told the spies that the people of the city were afraid of the Israelites. When soldiers came looking for the spies, she hid them and helped them escape. In exchange, the Israelites agreed to spare Rahab and her family.

After Jericho was captured, Rahab married into the family that was the line from which Jesus would come. It is interesting to note that one of Jesus' ancestors was a non-Jewish woman of ill repute.

PERIOD OF THE JUDGES

When the people had settled in the land of Canaan, they had no government. As long as the people sought God, they prospered. When their hearts turned away, they would fall victim to the nations around them. When this happened, God would raise up leaders to deliver the people and turn the nation back to Him. These people were called Judges. There were about 13 Judges during this time recorded in the Bible.

Some of the most notable Judges were **Deborah, Samson, Jephthah, Gideon,** and **Samuel**. The judges seem to have had varying roles. **Samson** was clearly not a spiritual leader. His exploits are more military in nature. **Deborah** was a Judge who was drafted into military leadership by the faithlessness of the military leader.

Gideon was a man who was found hiding in a wine press. When God called on him to lead the Israelites in battle, Gideon put God to a few tests. (Make the ground wet and the fleece dry and vice-versa.)

God used Gideon but went to great lengths to ensure that He (God) would get the credit. It was very important to God that Israel did not think that they had delivered themselves by their own strength. Israel had an army of 32,000 men but that was too many. God had Gideon get the number of men down to 300 before engaging the enemy. Gideon became a national hero but this praise went to his head. He built an ephod, which was a kind of idol, and all of the people prostituted themselves before it. It became a snare to Gideon and his family.

It is interesting to study the events of Gideon's life. He was a humble man in the beginning, but by the end he leads the entire nation down an idolatrous path.

Samuel was a spiritual leader, a prophet, and a Judge. He was the last of the Judges and it was during his time that the nation of Israel demanded a king. They wanted to be like all of the nations around them. Samuel felt that he had been rejected by the people, but God told Samuel that it was not he who had been rejected, but it was God Himself whom Israel rejected as their King.

It was some time during the period of the Judges that the events of the **Book of Ruth** occurred.

This book describes the plight of a Hebrew family that had moved to Moab. The wife's name was Naomi. She had two sons who married Moabite women. In time, her husband and both sons died. Her daughters-in-law were both still young, so she encouraged them to stay with their people and remarry. One of them, Ruth, would not. She vowed to stay with Naomi wherever she went.

Naomi and Ruth returned to Israel where Ruth attracted the attention of, and eventually married, a man named Boaz. King David is a direct descendant of Boaz and Ruth. Thus, Jesus is also a direct descendant of Ruth, a Gentile.

THE UNITED KINGDOM
(1 Samuel, 2 Samuel and 1 Kings 1-11)

The period of time that includes the reigns of King Saul, King David and King Solomon, is referred to as the United Kingdom.

When the Israelites demanded a king, God went to great lengths to tell them all that would go wrong as a result of having a king. Because their hearts were set on being like all of the nations around them, God relented and selected Saul to be the nation's first king. In the beginning, he was a good leader.

Saul was anointed king and led the nation for 40 years. At some point, Saul began to turn away from following the Lord and things began to go badly for the nation. It seems there is a lesson to be learned in this. God will sometimes give you or allow you to have things that are not in your best interest. The Israelites wanted a king. God said that is not such a good idea. They persisted. He relented. You see the result. The nation is in turmoil.

When Saul began to turn away from following the Lord, God had Samuel go to the house of Jesse and anoint David as the next king. David was not made king at this time but was designated to take Saul's place. Several years would pass before David would become king. This anointing was kept secret from Saul.

It was during the reign of Saul that Goliath taunted the armies of Israel. No one had the courage to fight Goliath until David, still a teenage boy, came to visit his brothers. David killed Goliath with nothing but a sling and a stone and then beheaded him. This strikes fear in the hearts of the Philistines and encourages the Israelites. The army of Israel wins a great victory as a result of David's courage and trust in God. In the course of time, David became a leader in Saul's army. He was a very close friend of Jonathan, King Saul's son.

As David's reputation grew and he became more and more popular with the people, Saul became jealous and began to fear that David would take his place as king. Saul tried to kill David, and David fled from him.

While he was in seclusion to avoid King Saul, a band of about 600 men gathered with David, and he became their leader. David twice had the opportunity to kill Saul, and thus presumably become king, but he would not take the life of the "Lord's anointed."

One day King Saul and his son Jonathan both died in battle. Saul took his own life when he was injured and could not escape. A messenger went to find David and told him that he had taken Saul's life. David had the messenger killed for killing the King.

Instead of running to seize power, David inquired of the Lord. He asked if he should go up to one of the cities in Israel. The Lord told him to go up to Hebron. David reigned for seven years over a small portion of the nation in Hebron. During these seven years, there was conflict between the house of Saul and the house of David. At the end of the seven years, the entire nation sent a delegation to David in Hebron asking him to come to Jerusalem and rule them.

It is interesting that the two greatest leaders of Israel (David and Moses) were not the kind of men that would seize power. I like to think that they were men who would take care of today's business and wait on the Lord to bring position to them.

PSALMS

During his life, David wrote many of the Psalms we have recorded. Several of them can be placed at various times or events in his life. Psalms is a book of songs, poems and meditations. They are not historical in nature but understanding the circumstances under which some of them were written gives us insight. This book would obviously be placed historically during the time frame covered in the books of 1st and 2nd Samuel.

A number of the psalms are clearly messianic (prophetic of the coming of Jesus). The New Testament authors treat them this way. Psalms 2, 16, 22, 68, 85, 110, 72, 45 and 144 are all considered to be messianic. There are other Psalms that may refer to Christ but these Psalms contain the most obvious references.

David had several wives and many children. It would be fair to say that he might not have been as good a parent as he should have been.

One day David saw Bathsheba, the wife of Uriah, one of his mighty men, bathing on the top of her roof. David had her brought to him, and she conceived a son. When David found out that she was pregnant, he tried to cover up his involvement. When that did not work, he had her husband killed in battle.

After the child was born to Bathsheba, God sent Nathan the prophet to David to convict him of his sin. David repented, yet a price had to be paid. The prophet told David that the sword would not leave his house.

From this point forward, David experienced many heartbreaking events:

The child born to David and Bathsheba died.

One of his sons raped one of his half sisters.

The whole brother of the sister killed the brother who raped his sister.

This same brother who killed his half brother led an almost successful revolt.

This brother, named Absalom, is killed by David's military leader, Joab.

It is fair to say that David paid for his sins many times over. Interestingly, God referred to David as *"a man after my own heart."* The lessons for us to take from the life of David are many. His life and walk with God deserve much study.

David had it in his heart to build the temple as a house for God. He was told that because he was such a "man of blood" that he would not build it himself but his son would. David stored up most of the needed materials so the temple could be built after his death.

David and Bathsheba had another son named Solomon. As it turns out, Solomon was to be the next king. When Solomon became king, he asked God for wisdom to rule the people. God granted his wish. Solomon was the wisest man who ever lived. Because he did not ask for long life, honor, power and wealth but instead asked for wisdom, God granted him wisdom and power and wealth.

Solomon developed an expansive kingdom. He built all kinds of projects, and everything he did prospered. It was he who built the temple. He also wrote the books of Proverbs, Ecclesiastes and The Song of Solomon.

Solomon is famous for having 700 wives and 300 concubines. Later in life, Solomon was led astray by his wives to serve other gods. It is not clear if he ever came back to serve the Lord.

ECCLESIASTES

Is a book devoted to wisdom and finding meaning in life. Solomon searched and tested everything for meaning. He built projects, he married women, he worked, he experienced leisure, he drank, and he ate.

He did everything he could think of in his search for meaning. Ecclesiastes 12:13-14 is his conclusion:

"Now all has been heard; here is the conclusion of the matter: Fear God and keep his commandments, for this is the whole duty of man. For God will bring every deed into judgment, including every hidden thing, whether it is good or evil."

Song of Solomon

Is the story of two lovers. Many people read this book as an allegory of God's love for his people. I am a little slow to embrace this idea. It could just be a love story.

Proverbs

Is a book that extols the virtue of wisdom. It contains many proverbs that have a wide range of applications.

The Divided Kingdom

The period from Solomon's death until the eventual fall of Israel is referred to as the Divided Kingdom

After Solomon's death, his son Rehoboam, became king. When he was to be appointed King,

Jeroboam, a political refugee who had fled Solomon and gone to live in Egypt, and a delegation went to speak to Rehoboam. They told him that Solomon had placed a heavy burden on the people to pay for all of his projects. They said if he would lighten the harsh labor and heavy yoke, they would serve Rehoboam. King Rehoboam asked the old men in his father's administration what to do. They told him that if he would be a servant to the people today and give them a favorable answer, in other words ease their burden; the people would always be his servants. Rehoboam did not listen. He took the advice of some of his friends who told him to make the burdens even greater.

The result of this tragic mistake was that Jeroboam led a revolt. Ten of the twelve tribes sided with Jeroboam and formed a new nation. The new nation kept the name Israel. This is the Northern Kingdom. The Southern Kingdom that remained loyal to Rehoboam was called Judah. The kingdom will never again be reunited.

The two nations followed similar patterns. They would live under a good king and turn back to God. God would bless them and things would go well. After the death of the good king, a king who did not serve God would rule, and the nation would go into decline.

During all of this, God sent prophets to preach to the people. There were many prophets who spoke to the nations at various times. Some were used in some specific ways with specific messages, but the overriding theme was that the people must turn and follow God, or He would bring judgment on them if they refused.

Eventually, God let the Northern Kingdom, called Israel, be completely destroyed forever by the Assyrians. Most of the people were not killed, but were taken captive, removed from the land, and assimilated into other civilizations. These 10 tribes were never to be heard from again. As with most things, it was not as simple and clear cut as this. No doubt, there were some God fearing Israelites that moved to Judah, and perhaps some were left in the land.

The Prophets

God often spoke to His people through messengers or "Prophets." Some prophets' careers were long, and their writings were voluminous. Others were used on a much more limited basis.

Major and minor prophets are classified based on the size of the book. The Major Prophets are Isaiah, Jeremiah, Ezekiel and Daniel. All of the others are considered minor.

Here is what we do not want to miss in the prophets. There are three categories of people who were "anointed." These are prophets, priests and kings. Jesus fulfills all three roles, and there are various prophecies that suggest the Messiah will be all three things.

It is important to recognize that there are multiple threads of messianic prophecy running throughout the Old Testament, and that they all culminate in the life of Christ.

1. King in the line of David
2. A Priest in the order of Melchizedek
3. A Prophet like Moses
4. A Great Shepherd for God's flock
5. A Suffering Servant
6. One like a Son of Man who will come on the clouds of heaven

The book of Isaiah is the record of the prophet by that name. Isaiah prophesied about many things related to Judah's unfaithfulness to God. He prophesied during the reign of four kings of Judah (Uzziah, Jotham, Ahaz and Hezekiah) about their eventual defeat by the Babylonians. Isaiah also prophesied about the Messiah. He is known as a messianic prophet because of this.

The Messiah (Hebrew word) is roughly equivalent to the Greek word for Christ. Both titles mean something like "anointed one," "deliverer," or "one who is coming." The idea for this great "deliverer" developed over time from the writings of the prophets but finds its origin in the promise that God made to Adam and Eve back in Genesis, Chapter 3. God promises all along to act decisively in the affairs of men to deliver them. The promises were taken by the Israelites to refer to physical or political deliverance, but the reality turns out to be that God delivers us from spiritual slavery and death. He accomplishes this in the person of Jesus.

Amos was a farmer when he was called by God to be a prophet. He was a prophet to Israel (Northern Kingdom and first to be conquered). He prophesied to Israel at the same time that Isaiah was a prophet to Judah.

Jonah was probably written by Jonah. It tells the story of a prophet whom God sent to a wicked Gentile nation called Assyria. Jonah at first ran away, was then thrown overboard, swallowed by a great fish, spit out on land, and finally went to speak as he had been commanded. He did it with a terrible attitude and got extremely angry when the people repented and were forgiven. This book teaches us a great deal about God's care and concern for all people. Many of the Jews could not conceive of the idea that God actually cares about Gentiles. In the last couple of verses of this book, God chastises Jonah and points out that there are over 120,000 people who do not know their right from their left and many cattle as well. *"Should I not be concerned about that great city?"* This ought to cause us to slow down to consider that God cares about everyone. Jonah did not care about 120,000 people made in the image of God. God thinks Jonah should care even about the cattle.

Hosea is a man of God with an unfaithful wife. He pursues and forgives her. This is the picture God wants the nation of Israel to see. It perfectly mirrors His relationship with Israel.

Joel was a prophet to the nation of Judah. He prophesies about the desolation of the land by a swarm of locusts followed by drought and famine. It is from Joel that the apostle Peter quotes when he explains why the apostles are able to speak in languages they do not know: Acts 2:14-21

Then Peter stood up with the Eleven, raised his voice and addressed the crowd: "Fellow Jews and all of you who live in Jerusalem, let me explain this to you; listen carefully to what I say. ¹⁵ These men are not drunk, as you suppose. It's only nine in the morning! ¹⁶ No, this is what was spoken by the prophet Joel: ¹⁷ "'In the last days, God says, I will pour out my Spirit on all people. Your sons and daughters will prophesy, your young men will see visions, your old men will dream dreams.[18] Even on my servants, both men and women, I will pour out my Spirit in those days, and they will prophesy.[19] I will show wonders in the heaven above and signs on the earth below, blood and fire and billows of smoke. [20] The sun will be turned to darkness and the moon to blood before the coming of the great and glorious day of the Lord. [21] And everyone who calls on the name of the Lord will be saved."[c]

Micah is one of the Minor Prophets who prophesy about the impending doom of Israel and Judah. Chapter 4 beautifully predicts the building of The Lord's House (the church) in the latter days.

Nahum, Habakkuk, Obadiah, Zephaniah, Zechariah and Malachi are all minor prophets with distinct messages.

Jeremiah was the last of God's messengers to Judah before it was finally conquered by Babylon. After Israel was taken over by the Assyrians, the nation of Judah continued for approximately another 135 years. God continued to send His prophets, but the nation would not repent. Eventually, God allowed Judah to be taken into captivity by the Babylonians. Jeremiah was a prophet to the nation of Judah right up to the time of their captivity. He escaped captivity and went to Egypt.

Lamentations are the laments of the Prophet Jeremiah. He spoke and wrote with such sorrow for the nations that he is known as the "weeping prophet."

Ezekiel was taken captive and prophesied to the people in Babylon. God did not abandon the nation even while they were in captivity. The events of the books of **Daniel and Esther** also occurred while the people were in captivity.

Esther is the story of how one faithful woman saved the Jews from annihilation while they were in exile. Once again, God proves faithful in delivering His people. Historically, this book would go after Kings / Chronicles and before Ezra and Nehemiah.

The book of Daniel is about a young man who was enslaved and taken to Babylon where he earned the trust of his captors and rose to some prominence in that nation. He could interpret dreams and some very interesting prophecies are recorded in this book. He interpreted a dream that foretold the rising of kingdoms, one after the other right up to the time that Jesus comes on the scene. Speaking of the time of the Roman Empire, Daniel says in Chapter 2, verse 44:

"In the time of those kings the God of heaven will set up a kingdom that will never be destroyed, nor will it be left to another people. It will crush all those

kingdoms and bring them to an end, but it will itself endure forever."

This is a reference to the Kingdom of God that will be preached by Jesus and established shortly after His resurrection.

The people were in captivity for about seventy years. By the time God was ready for the nation of Judah to return to their homeland, Babylon had been taken over by the Medes and the Persians. God worked through them to bring about the peaceful return of the Jews to their homeland.

Some of the people came home, but not all of them did. The scattering of the Jewish people throughout the Mediterranean World as a result of the exiles is commonly called the Diaspora, from a Greek word meaning "scattering" or "dispersal". The ones who did return found the temple destroyed, the walls of the city torn down, and the people living in the land worshiping other gods.

The book of Haggai tells us how Haggai the prophet inspired the people to rebuild the temple.

The book of Ezra tells us about the rebuilding of the temple and reinstatement of the Law.

The book of Nehemiah is the story of how the wall around Jerusalem was rebuilt as the people were returning to Jerusalem. This is a great book to study the subject of leadership.

Once the nation was reestablished, Judah once again has trouble remaining faithful to God.

Malachi, the last book of the Old Testament, ends with the promise that Elijah would come before the Day of the Lord.

The Intertestamental Period

Note: This period is not recorded in the Bible. I include it here to help develop a sense of history.

After God speaks to the people through Malachi, the nation of Judah would exist for around four hundred years with no direct word from God. This is the period between the Old and the New Testaments. It is commonly referred to as the Intertestamental Period.

The Jews had been allowed to return, but only a small portion of them actually came back to their homeland. Here they did not enjoy political freedom and were continually under the yoke of one foreign power or another. After they returned from captivity, they were still subject to the Persians. Later, they found themselves under the control of the Greeks. While the Jewish people were subject to the Greek Empire, they were forced to pay tribute, and there was an intense effort to Hellenize them, or make them Greek, which was resented deeply.

It was in this setting that a Jewish priest named Mathias Ben Johanan killed a Jew, who had offered a sacrifice to a pagan god, along with a Greek soldier. He was forced to flee to the desert with his five sons. In the desert, he formed a band of rebels and died within a year or so. Mathias' third son Judas became the leader of this band of rebels. Judas was a fiery, passionate and effective leader. He was nicknamed Maccabee, which means "hammer" (for hammering the enemy). The group became known as "The Maccabees". They were successful to some extent, and the nation won a degree of freedom for a period of time. Hanukkah is a Jewish holiday, still celebrated today, that remembers these achievements.

Even with the success of "The Maccabees", the Jews could not stop the Romans from seizing control of them in 163 B.C. The Jews lived with appointed Governors and High Priests, and once again resented it deeply. Later the Romans appointed Herod King of the Jews, and they resented him even more because he was not really Jewish and only pretended to be. They longed all the more for that great redemptive act of God that had been spoken of by the prophets so long ago.

In an effort to remain faithful and separate themselves from the others in the land, the Jews created the synagogues.

They held to several fundamental beliefs.
1.   Monotheism—there is but one God.
2.   Election—He had chosen them (the Jews) from among all people.
3.   God gave them the law to govern their lives.
4.   The land was holy (The land their nation occupied was given them by God).
5.   Hope for a future redemptive act.

It was during this time that the sects of the Jews developed.

The Pharisees are one of these groups. They wanted to separate Israel from the pagan Greek influence and believed in radical obedience to the Torah.

The Essenes were another group that developed during this time. They objected to the culture but unlike the Pharisees, were not content to work within it. They isolated themselves and lived in what we might call a commune.

The Sadducees, yet another group were the official teachers of the law and the recognized leaders of the temple. They were politically connected and got along well with the Romans. This group did not believe in angels or the resurrection of the dead.

The Zealots, a fourth group, were a subculture of nationalists who wanted above all to rid the nation of its rulers. They were in favor of violent revolution.

Those not belonging to any of these groups were the common people. Most of the Jews were not associated with any group.

The New Testament

It was into this feverish political and religious environment that Jesus is born. The story of His birth must be seen in the context of the national hope of the Jewish people at that time. God sends His answer to sin and bondage in the person of Jesus. He is renewing all things and restoring them to Himself, but Jesus is not recognized by most of the people.

The story of the life of Jesus is told in the four gospels (**Matthew, Mark, Luke and John**). Matthew, Mark and Luke are very similar and cover much of the same material. These are known as the synoptic gospels. The gospel of John is unique and tells the story of Jesus' life in a very different way.

In fulfillment of Old Testament prophecy, Jesus is born to a young virgin named Mary. She was pledged to be married to Joseph. When Joseph discovered that Mary was pregnant, he made plans to *"put her away,"* but he was told by an angel that the baby was from the

Lord. Joseph decided not to divorce Mary, and he and Mary traveled to Bethlehem to be counted in the Roman census. While they were there, Jesus was born in a stable. Angels announced the birth of Jesus to shepherds who were nearby. They came to see and worship Jesus.

When Jesus was twelve years old, His family inadvertently left Him in Jerusalem and headed back home. They assumed He was with other family members. When they went to look for him, they found Him in the temple discussing the scriptures with those around Him.

Jesus had a cousin named John. John started preaching repentance for the forgiveness of sins and gained many converts. He was the one that had been mentioned in the Old Testament who would prepare the way for the Lord. He also fulfilled the prophecy that Elijah would come before the Day of the Lord. It seems his role was to prepare the hearts of the people to hear Jesus. John baptized his followers and was referred to as John the Baptist (or Baptizer).

John the Baptist was a great teacher. Inspired by God, he recognized Jesus as the promised one, and he called him the *"Lamb of God."* What we want to catch is that it was innocent lambs that were slain during the Jewish Passover. John was saying that Jesus is the true Lamb who would provide deliverance for

God's people. It appears that many, but not all, of John's disciples left him to follow Jesus. Even after John's death, his teachings continued to have great impact with pockets of followers existing throughout the Roman world.

Jesus began His public ministry at the age of thirty. Even though Jewish boys underwent a bar mitzvah and became subject to the Law at age thirteen, thirty was the generally recognized age of full maturity in Jewish culture. It would not have been possible for Jesus to call disciples and to be recognized generally as a practicing rabbi before this age. His ministry only lasted about three years. He called twelve men to be his apostles. These men stayed with Him essentially the entire time for the three years of His ministry.

The ministry of Jesus is highlighted by His frequent teachings on the Kingdom of God, by His healing all sorts of illnesses, by His casting out of demons, and by His teaching through parables. Another feature of all the gospel accounts is a long running conflict with the Pharisees, Sadducees and Teachers of the Law. These groups were the established religious leaders during the life of Jesus.

The core teachings of Jesus were centered on the Kingdom of God, the corruption of the Law by religious leaders, and the fact that He was the one who was to come. He taught his disciples that He is the Son of God and that He and The Father are one. In one of his more poignant statements (John 14:6), Jesus says:

"I am the way and the truth and the life, no one comes to the Father except through me."

If the weight of this one statement could be grasped, people would be well on the way to religious and spiritual clarity. It all comes down to whether or not Jesus is telling us the truth. Do you believe this one thing or do you not? If you believe this statement, you cannot believe the idea that there are many paths to God. If you do not believe this statement, you simply do not believe the words of Jesus.

Jesus came to live without sin and to offer His perfect life in exchange for ours. In doing so, He also taught us how to live.

It is evident that His apostles did not fully grasp all that Jesus taught even though they were with Him night and day for three years.

Large portions of the gospels record the events of the last week of Jesus' life. Jesus was ultimately slain during Passover as the true Lamb of God. The Jews handed Him over to the Roman authorities who found no fault with Him. At the Jews' insistence, the Romans crucified Jesus. He died on a cross as a sacrifice for our sins. Anyone in any age who is saved is saved only because of what God did on the cross through Jesus. This includes all of our Old Testament heroes, those of us in the church today, and anyone God might decide to save in the future.

The significance of what happened on the cross cannot be overstated. Every human being who ever lived or ever will live is or will be guilty of sin. Jesus bore all of our guilt on the cross. As He bore the curses, darkness settled over the land, the earth shook and rocks split. But by dying, Jesus delivered us from every curse. It is plain enough to see that Jesus was *smitten by God and afflicted*" (Isaiah 53:4).

The crucifixion is God's fury, His wrath and His justice reaching its climax. In the death of His Son, God Himself feels what it means to die under the curse. God is no longer a stranger to sin and death. This is not an impersonal, sterile transaction. His death was not just a cold, academic "accounting" for sin. It does not stoop to the petty vindictiveness that is so common to man. God the Father stands in opposition to God the Son. No theology, no reasoning, no ram caught in a thicket can swoop in and save the day. There simply is no way out. As God's wrath is satisfied, the earth trembles, the sun fades away. This is the horrible judgment of the Living God. No wonder darkness shrouds the land as Jesus asks;

"Why have you forsaken me?"

What a terrible scene. Christ, the sinless one, faced the full wrath of God for and because of me. And yet, what a beautiful scene this is. We are freed from the curse and have gained access into the presence of God. *"Righteousness and peace kissed that day."* (Psalm 85:10)

At this point, you might be asking why Jesus had to die for our sins. Why could God not just "let it go" and forgive people who repented? This is a good question that deserves an answer. My best answer is that just as God is light and love, He is also just. God has instructed us not to convict the innocent or acquit the guilty. Even our own skewed sense of justice demands that our Judges convict the guilty. The point is that God, being just, could not overlook sin and remain just. Paul comments on this very subject in Romans 3:25-26:

"God presented him as a sacrifice of atonement through faith in his blood. He did this to demonstrate his justice, because in his forbearance he had left the sins committed beforehand unpunished—he did it to demonstrate his justice at the present time, so as to be

just and the one who justifies those who have faith in Jesus."

After Jesus was crucified, Joseph of Arimathea went to Pilate and gained permission to take Jesus' body and place it in a tomb. The Jews were concerned that someone might steal the body and asked the Romans to place a guard at the tomb.

On the first day of the week, some women went to anoint Jesus' body for burial, but when they arrived, the stone over the entrance to the tomb had been removed and Jesus was not there. He had risen. Jesus appeared to several of His disciples at various times. At His last appearance, He told the Apostles to:

"go and make disciples of all nations, baptizing them in the name of the Father, and of the Son and of the Holy Spirit and teaching them to obey everything I have commanded you." Matthew 28:19-20

Jesus then ascended into Heaven.

THE ACTS OF THE APOSTLES (ACTS)

Fifty days after Passover (when Jesus was crucified), during the feast of Pentecost, the Holy Spirit descended on the twelve Apostles. They started preaching in languages they did not know.

People nearby accused them of being drunk. Peter stood up and preached the **Gospel** (good news about Jesus) for the first time. Peter convinced many that they were guilty of sin including shedding the blood of the Son of God. About three thousand were baptized that day. The Kingdom of God has now been established on earth. There is a great deal of teaching about the Kingdom of God that can be confusing. There is no doubt that there is some sense in which the Kingdom is still to come, but it is certain that there is also a sense in which it has come and is in and among us.

People from many nations were in Jerusalem for the celebration of Pentecost. When they heard about Jesus, believed and were converted, they naturally wanted to stay in the city for an extended period of time. This caused the people who lived locally to begin selling land and possessions in order to provide for the needs of the believers from out of town. The church grew each day.

At this point the church was pretty much a local phenomenon. Then, in Acts, Chapter 7, we read about the stoning of a devout Christian named Stephen. On that same day, a great persecution broke out against the church at Jerusalem. The Christians were scattered throughout Judea and Samaria, and they preached the word wherever they went.

A few years later, the church was still comprised of Jews and converts to Judaism. In Acts, Chapter 10, we read of the first Gentile convert to Christianity. The Bible says that Cornelius was a devout, God fearing Gentile who prayed regularly and gave alms to the poor. An angel appeared to Cornelius and told him to send for Peter. The apostle did come to the home of Cornelius even though it was unthinkable for a Jew to go to the home of a Gentile, and Peter told all of those assembled about Jesus. Cornelius and all of those in his house were baptized in the name of Jesus.

This story is significant for several reasons. It does highlight the first Gentile converts and Peter's prejudice, but above all the story is about God accepting men from all nations who fear Him and want to do what is right. This is really good news. The gospel is not for the Jews alone. God loves and accepts us Gentiles as well.

The idea of God bringing together all nations to worship him is sprinkled throughout the Old Testament beginning with God's promise to Abraham that all nations will be blessed through his offspring. Yet the story of Cornelius makes it clear that even Jesus' closest disciples did not really "get" the full significance of the very enterprise entrusted to their care! In the first chapters of Acts they were focused on presenting Jesus as the promised Messiah to the nation of Israel. It seems not to have dawned on them that Jesus came to open the door to God for all mankind.

New Testament (Christian) theology seems to have developed only slowly as Peter, Paul, John and others work out the full significance of Jesus' life, death, burial and resurrection over a number of decades in the early church. The notion that all the Apostles rejected Judaism and suddenly became Christians on the Day of Pentecost is contradicted not only by the text but also by the evidence of history and human nature that old prejudices die hard. One could argue that God had to figuratively hit Peter over the head with a hammer, and Peter's astonishment at the house of Cornelius is enough to explain why God had to do so.

In Acts, Chapter 9, we read about the conversion of a Jewish leader who ruthlessly persecuted the church. Saul of Tarsus was traveling from city to city seeking out Christians to persecute and even put them to death. Jesus appeared to Saul while he was on his way to Damascus to persecute the Christians there. Saul was converted and became the most prolific evangelist and Christian writer. Essentially the entire second half of the book of Acts is dedicated to Paul's (formerly Saul) travels as he preached the good news of Jesus and started churches in many cities. Paul considered it his special task to serve as "Apostle to the Gentiles" (Romans 11:13, Galatians 2:7). It is during these travels described in Acts that he wrote many of the letters to the churches that make up much of the rest of the New Testament. The book of Acts closes with Paul in prison in Rome, presumably awaiting execution.

THE EPISTLES

The next several "books" of the New Testament are known as the "epistles" or letters to individuals or churches. Paul did not write them all, but he did write the majority of them.

The letter to the Romans was written by Paul to the church at Rome. This letter is a masterpiece of theology. In it, Paul wrote to a church that was comprised of Jewish and Gentile believers. He persuasively argued that Gentiles and Jews alike are all utterly sinful and without hope except for faith in Christ and the faithfulness of God. We need righteousness to stand before God. He argued that righteousness is not obtained by circumcision, by being Jewish, by keeping the law, or by good works. The only way to obtain righteousness is to seek it by faith. Those who are made righteous by faith will live (have life). Remember that "Abraham believed God and it was credited to him as righteousness."

First and Second Corinthians are letters Paul wrote to the church at Corinth. The church had numerous issues. They had disorderly worship, people were suing each other in the public courts, they had divisions in the church and they easily tolerated gross sexual immorality. These letters were written to address the problems in Corinth, and they contain a wealth of practical Christian teaching. The encouraging thing is that Paul addressed them as *"the church of God at Corinth."* Even with all of the issues, Paul still considered them the church. Of course, we cannot in any way use this thinking to allow ourselves to become complacent in our walk with God.

Galatians is a letter written by Paul to the churches in Galatia. This letter was written to combat some teaching that had crept into the church. Some Jewish Christians had convinced some in Galatia that they must be circumcised and obey at least parts of the Jewish Law in order to be Christians. Paul strongly condemned this teaching and stressed his point that if they turned to the Law, they were turning to worthless principles and risked falling from grace.

Ephesians was written by Paul to the church in Ephesus. Paul highlighted the fact that it is God doing the work in salvation and that he has prepared good works that we should do. This letter also contains an abundance of instruction in Christian living.

Philippians was written by Paul to the church at Philippi. Paul stressed living a joy-filled life while writing from prison.

Colossians was written by Paul to the church at Colossae. This letter addresses salvation and Christian living.

First and Second Thessalonians were both written by Paul to the church at Thessalonica. Both letters are very short and address the coming of the Lord.

First and Second Timothy were written by Paul to his "son in the faith" Timothy. Paul had trained Timothy as an evangelist. These letters were intended to remind Timothy of some of the things he was taught and to further instruct him.

Titus is a letter written by Paul to Titus, another evangelist. As with Timothy, Paul was reminding and encouraging Titus in his work.

Philemon was written by Paul to a Christian brother. Paul had converted Philemon's runaway slave to Christ and was sending him back to his master. The point of the letter was to encourage Philemon to treat his slave Onesimus as a brother. One of the fundamental tenets of Christianity is the equality of believers.

The writer of **Hebrews** is unknown. Many think it was written by Paul. Others believe either Barnabas or Apollos wrote it. Whoever the author was, he must have been a great church leader in a position of authority. It clearly was written to Jews to prove the absolute superiority of Jesus, and to encourage them not to return to Judaism.

James was written by Jesus' brother James to the church at large. He addressed it to the "twelve tribes" (very Jewish) "scattered among the nations." Without getting stuck on the intended audience, it is a very practical book with some challenging teachings.

First and Second Peter were written by Peter to the Christians scattered about. These letters are filled with practical instructions for living as a Christian.

First, Second and Third John were written by the apostle John who also wrote the fourth gospel.

Jude was written by Jude, the Lord's brother. He called himself the brother of James but did not identify himself as the brother of Jesus.

Revelation is the final book of the New Testament. The author identified himself as John, but the book is *"the revelation of Jesus Christ, which God gave Him to show His servants what must soon take place."*

(Revelation 1:1) The next sentence says that *"He made it known by sending his angel to His servant John."* So, you could say that Jesus wrote it.

John was in exile on the Island of Patmos when he received the revelation. This book is written in a style of literature (Apocalyptic) that was common for its time but is very foreign to us. This explains, at least in part, why the message of this book is so difficult to grasp.

Early in the book, Jesus dictates letters to seven churches in Asia. These letters were church specific and teaching from these letters should be done with great care and caution today. Without a doubt, this is a difficult book. Many claim to have it mastered, but most of them read it as if it were entirely about future events. There is a great deal of evidence that supports the idea that it was in large part a message to the Christians of that century to not give up, keep the faith, because in the end, they would overcome.

The reality was and is that Christ has already overcome. We know the score at the end of the game. Yet, the game is still being played. We win, so don't give up.

Perhaps after reading this you are inclined to think the story is not "all that simple." Here it is:

God created mankind and had fellowship with them. They sinned and fellowship was broken. The rest of the Bible tells the story of how God took it upon Himself to redeem His people through the death of Jesus on the cross.

Another way to sum up the teaching of the Bible is found in John 3:16-17

"For God so loved the world that He gave His one and only Son that whoever believes in Him shall not perish but have eternal life. For God did not send His son into the world to condemn the world but to save the world through Him."

It really is that simple.

Printed in the United States
By Bookmasters